Otto Oeder

Along the Border

On patrol at the Iron Curtain

Bibliographic information of the German National Library: The German National Library lists this publication in the German National Bibliography; detailed bibliographic data are available on the Internet at dnb.dnb.de.

© 2022 Otto Oeder

Production and Publisher:
BoD - Books on Demand, Norderstedt, Germany.

ISBN 9783756852413

Table of contents

Foreword

God did not want the author to be born a war child, which is why He waited until May 13, 1945, when the armistice had just been signed by the victorious powers, but weapons were still smoking from time to time and the Americans had just taken up quarters in his central Franconian market town of Markt Erlbach opposite his birthplace in the old district court. This meant for his parents and him from the beginning a hard future full of privation.

At the beginning he had neither shoes nor a school bag for school. It was not until the mid-fifties that things got better for him and he was able to earn some of his own food, at least by working for farmers as a child. He was denied the opportunity to attend high school because his parents could not afford the travel costs to the city 30 kilometers away or the books and exercise books. Therefore, at the age of 14, he had to leave home and learn the butcher's trade in another village, where he had board and lodgings and was no longer dependent on his parents. This tough childhood shaped him in such a way that he vowed to move up the ladder someday where he would have an easier time. His chance came when he applied to the Bavarian riot police and, after passing the recruitment test, was allowed to "move in" to the barracks in Würzburg on March 9, 1964.

After completing his training as a police officer, he reported to the border police station at Bad Steben in the Franconian Forest, right next to the Iron Curtain, in 1967. There, until the fall of the Wall in 1989, he performed border and general police duties on the "death strip" and received many a GDR refugee in Bavaria. The most joyful event, however, was the opening of the border, where he was present at several provisional border crossings in construction vehicles, which served as duty posts, and was able to experience how the Iron Curtain became more and more porous. In mid-1990, his post was renamed the Bavarian State Police Station. There he served as chief commissioner until his retirement in 2006.

I have written this book for my family, friends and acquaintances, and especially for my grandchildren, so that they can find out how a little "rascal" became a "border guard" at the "Iron Curtain" in the middle of Germany.

Childhood and upbringing

In 1945, when the Americans still occupied Thuringia and Saxony, I was born four days after the armistice in Markt Erlbach in Middle Franconia as the second child of a day laborer couple. After that, two more siblings saw the light of day in our small two-room rented apartment.

Until we left school, we grew up poor and modest, but well protected. Already as an eleven-year-old I was given to a farmer's family to work there for food and housing. There I had to do stable work early in the morning, even before school started, and field and forest work after school, and in the evening I had to do my homework on the side. I was not allowed to go to school sports in the afternoon, because working was more important. After I was beaten by the farmer's wife with a whip on my naked upper body because of something trivial (I was supposed to get off a cart with two cows, which was not fast enough for the farmer's wife), I ran away barefoot and fearfully went back to my parents, because I did not know whether I would be welcome at home or not. But thank God, they took their "prodigal son" back.

In the summer months we gathered dry wood and spruce cones in the forest or helped our parents with "digging sticks", collecting blueberries and forest mushrooms and for the tea in winter we picked lime blossoms and chamomile blossoms. In addition, we provided more than 20 rabbits with the necessary food, which we "plucked" by hand from meadows or fields and had to be careful that the farmers did not see us.

Apprenticeships

At the age of 14, I was "promised" by my parents to a master butcher in another town as an apprentice. After the school dismissal service in July 1959, the master butcher was already waiting in front of the church and took me with him. There I learned this trade for three years and came home to my family only once or twice a year. After successfully passing the journeyman's examination, I looked for work in my profession in the nearest large city and started working in a large butcher shop. In mid-1963, after my 18th birthday, I became aware of an advertisement from the Bavarian Riot Police asking for police recruits. At the time, I was due to be drafted into the German Armed Forces, so I applied for police service.

In the fall of 1963, I was then ordered to a two-day entrance examination at a barracks of the Bavarian Riot Police in Nuremberg. Of the eleven examinees, ten were high school students and of course I was the only one with 8 grades of elementary school and a journeyman's certificate as a butcher. After the written examinations on the first day, five candidates were sent home immediately because they had not passed the examination. The rest were allowed to stay and had to pass the sports, medical and oral exams the next day. After passing these last exams, I was already told that I would be allowed to "move in" to the police accommodation in Würzburg in March 1964. On March 9, I took the train to Würzburg and stood there at the station as an eighteen-year-old with my few belongings in a cardboard box and the draft notice quite poorly. But I knew how to help myself and had a cab take me to the police barracks. After dressing in uniforms, underwear and even a nightgown, I was taken to the barracks. The new arrivals were assigned to the individual platoons. I was assigned to the V-bike platoon, which is why I had to start training for my motorcycle license immediately after basic training and was also assigned a police "BMW machine" after passing the test.

The Author as a Kradmelder in 1964 in the Police Accommodation in Würzburg

II/1   63 130549

L a n d e s a m t   8 München 37, den 15. 1. 1964
für die   Albolfach
Bayerische Bereitschaftspolizei   Arcisstraße 19

Herrn

Otto   O e d e r
8551   Markt Erlbach üb.Neust.Aisch
       Windsheimer Straße 29

Betreff: Einberufung in die Bayer. Bereitschaftspolizei

Sehr geehrter Herr Oeder!

        Sie werden hiermit zur Dienstleistung bei der
Bayer. Bereitschaftspolizei einberufen und gebeten, sich

        im Laufe des 9. März 1964, spätestens bis 17 Uhr

        in der Polizeiunterkunft Würzburg, Ysenburgstr.1,

einzufinden.

        Sie werden in den Polizeidienst einberufen unter
dem Vorbehalt des Ergebnisses einer polizeiärztlichen Nach-
untersuchung und unter der Voraussetzung, daß sich bis zum
Einstellungstermin keine Tatsachen ergeben, die Sie für eine
Verwendung in der Bayerischen Bereitschaftspolizei unge-
eignet erscheinen lassen.

        Über Ihre Bezüge erhalten Sie eine gesonderte Mit-
teilung. Der erste Unterhaltszuschuß wird aus kassentech-
nischen Gründen erst eine Woche nach Dienstantritt ausbezahlt
werden können.

An Papieren sind   Zur Ergänzung Ihrer Unterla-
noch mitzubringen: gen sind weiterhin vorzulegen:

1. Steuerkarte,
2. Reisepaß oder Bundes-
   personalausweis,   ————————
3. Fahrkarte,

soweit vorhanden:

4. Flüchtlingsausweis
5. Führerschein.

                                                        -/-

Draft order 1964

11

After that, I had to take my class 3 police driver's license for official cars. On weekdays, from 8 a.m. to 5 p.m., there were lessons in traffic law, criminal and civil service law, civics and other subjects. Special emphasis was placed on shooting, sports, self-defense, boxing, and swimming.

Every Wednesday, however, we went out on our motorcycles to the Rhön or the Spessart and were trained as motorcycle spotters or in traffic accident reporting. When we returned to our home barracks in the evening, we looked in our motorcycle suits as if we had just returned from a campaign. From top to bottom we were full of dirt and sand and the grains of sand crunched between our teeth. Tired and still fully dressed, we took a shower together with our motorcycle clothes, because the next day was roll call and everything had to be clean again. After such a ride, we fell asleep silently in our eight-bed room. Alone because of lack of oxygen, because the next morning you could "cut" the air.

Lunch break somewhere in the Spessart

At the same time, I had to take the typing and stenography exams. If you failed just one of these exams, everything was for nothing and you were discharged within 14 days without any ifs or buts, which I wanted to avoid, of course, because I knew how hard it was out there in the working world and the barracks had become my surrogate parental home. Here I had everything I needed: food, drink, friends and comrades. I swore to myself, "You'll stick with it here," and studied and studied as much as I could so that I would get good grades on the intermediate exams.

A fateful internship

After more than 3 years, I then successfully passed the final examinations for the intermediate police civil service. During my training in 1965, I was assigned to a three-month internship at the then Bavarian border police station in Lichtenberg in the Franconian Forest, where I was able to get to know the first steps in field service at the "East Zone border". The double patrols were carried out day and night along the zone border mainly on foot in all weathers. The old "border guards" with world war experience learned me first of all how to "walk on patrol" by giving me the tip that one had to walk in such a way that the tips of the coats were not allowed to move. At night, we could hear the border guards of the National People's Army of the East Zone talking in their earth bunkers in the woods, because the distance to them was often only about 5 to 25 meters due to the landscape.

Along our service area there were many natural water borders between Bavaria and the "Iron Curtain", e.g. the Thuringian and Franconian rivers Muschwitz, Selbitz and Saale.

First snowfall in October 1965, on the left the author in front of the patrol car on the market square in Lichtenberg

Since the Bavarian border police did not have portable radios at that time and we therefore had no contact to our police station while on patrol (which was sometimes a good thing), we had to keep to "point times", i.e. we had to approach certain, mostly prominent points in the landscape and had to position ourselves there for about 30 minutes. Only there another patrol or the duty officer could meet us and control us, which often happened. Woe betide us if we didn't keep to these times. That was almost like a guard misdemeanor.

Some of these locations were very good for us. One of them was in a small town with only one pub.

We had to position ourselves right in front of this pub. When the chief of police arrived with the VW Beetle police car for the inspection, we could already see a cloud of dust coming towards us from far away, because the road to this place had not yet been paved. So we calmly stood in front of the pub and quietly waited to see what might come. After our report to the superior officer "No special incidents", he drove away satisfied and we could return to the warm and dry pub.

Of course, we had good contact with the population in the foot border service and received many a tip and hint from them, which has unfortunately been lost in modern times. I learned right away that three things are important for the police profession, namely "seeing, hearing and communicating with the population". These three months of internship with the border police in the Franconian Forest had such an impact on me that I was considering to switch to this police organization after my training, because dealing with the locals and the community was so much fun and the nature really appealed to me. Under no circumstances did I want to become a city policeman, e.g. in Munich.

In addition, I met and fell in love with a "Frankenwald girl" during this time, which of course also influenced my thoughts and later decision to join the border police.

Then in the fall of 1965 the time came when the internship was over and I had to say goodbye to my colleagues of the Bavarian Border Police, my girlfriend and the wonderful Franconian Forest.

Having matured a bit, I returned to warmer climes to my police accommodation in Würzburg, where the daily routine of training took its course again.

Even before the end of the training and the final exams, so-called "recruiters" for the rural, municipal, water protection, riot and border police were already "sneaking" around in the barracks area to recruit us to their associations. Although they offer the most beautiful gifts, such as low-cost rental state apartments at the place of duty or service on the motorboat of the water police on Lake Constance or the Rhine-Main-Danube Canal or with the border police at Munich Airport or border service at the Austrian border in the Alps. I decided to serve at the border in the Franconian Forest and applied for a job at the Bad Steben border police station. After passing the test, I left Würzburg in my old 1954 VW Beetle for the Franconian Forest. I had all my belongings with me: a loose-leaf collection of laws, an Olympia portable typewriter, which I had had to buy for 420 DM, equivalent to two months' salary, to learn how to type, and what clothes I owned. That was all I had, but I did have the promise of a secure job as a probationary civil servant.

Former railroad line interrupted by border demarcation near Lichtenberg, Blechschmiedtenhammer.

Starting Work life

In June 1967 I started my service at the border police station Bad Steben, directly at the "Iron Curtain", as a fully trained police officer and one month later I married my girlfriend and fiancée from the same place.

A year later, while I was obviously on night duty, our son was born at home and I was not there. Two years later, I was there at the birth of our daughter and was the "right hand man" of the midwife. So I had to heat water on the stove, etc. Our children then naturally grew up with this terrible border.

Not much had changed in terms of duty and the patrols were still mainly done on foot, but the department already had a VW Beetle without radio as a patrol car, but it was rarely used. The fuel allocation for it was about 150 liters per month with an average consumption of 20 liters per 100 km short distance. Since we were only allowed to drive up to 20 km on a 6-hour patrol, it was not possible to keep the patrol car reasonably warm in the winter. But we were inventive and had a crossroads outside Bad Steben, where very rarely anyone passed by. There we put the car in reverse and drove around in circles. The speedometer actually rewound the kilometers driven and it became pleasantly warm in the car, but of course the fuel consumption increased enormously. The older colleague, who then did the gasoline bill at the end of the month, was surprised every time that the VW Beetle had "drunk" so much again.

In 1967, the author was on patrol at the zone border near Krötenmühle, Bad Steben. Behind it, the Muschwitz border stream and the mined death strip.

At that time, we carried our 7.65 mm pistol, a 9 mm submachine gun, nightsticks and handcuffs. During foot patrols, we also carried a report bag with search documents, etc. Customs, the Federal Border Guard and the U.S. Army were also on duty to secure the border. At certain intervals, we drove double patrols together with the Americans in their jeeps, which provided a lot of variety. They also provided us with night vision equipment, which allowed us to spot people or animals in the pitch dark and approach the border in the patrol car even without lights. During one such night patrol, a woman came running towards us from the direction of the border at the edge of a small village around midnight. Since she looked suspicious to us and had a somewhat southern appearance, we stopped her. When we asked her what she was doing in the middle of the night in the customs border area, she said she had gone to the communal cold store in the village to quickly get a roast pork. Since we did not want to believe her at such a late hour and she could not identify herself, we arrested her and drove her to her apartment. There, her husband confirmed the woman's claims and, after establishing her identity beyond doubt by checking her ID card, the "arrest" was stopped. It should be noted that persons staying in the "customs border area" could be checked at any time and without reason. The "customs border area" was a strip along the zone border with a depth of 30 km and the word "customs border area" could be read on every place name sign.

The Inner-German border

We were responsible for general police duties, i.e., to prevent and prosecute criminal offences or violations and to avert danger, and we were also tasked with monitoring the zone border. If, for example, we had to deal with a traffic accident, a burglary, a suicide or even just "domestic violence," we were "rural police officers," and if a refugee came to meet us or we noticed an incident at the zone border or a border violation, we were "border guards.

When I started here, there were only two rows of "Spanish horsemen" with barbed wire parallel to the border, 20 to 30 meters apart, and a 10-meter-wide control strip. The intermediate area was secured by explosive and fragmentation mines, which went up when pressure was applied or when thinly stretched wires were passed through, in order to stop the "border violator". At certain intervals, earth observation pillboxes camouflaged with brushwood were hidden in the countryside. They were used for covert observation of the terrain on both sides of the border.

In order to stop escapes by cars or trucks, a motor vehicle moat was built in 1966. Through this approx. 1.50 m wide trench with sloping concrete slabs, this escape route was also eliminated. At the same time, the column road, which had been unpaved until then, was paved with concrete slabs and a three-meter-high mesh fence was gradually erected. Directly behind it ran the 6-meter-wide, harrowed control road, which had to be walked along during each patrol in order to determine whether a shoeprint of a fugitive was present. Since no mines had been laid along the banks of the Selbitz River in Blankenstein because of the nearby buildings - the inhabited houses being directly on the border - a 3-meter-high concrete wall with a concrete pipe on top (the same construction as the Berlin Wall) was built by sappers of the border troops instead of the metal fence. Along this wall dog runs with shepherd dogs were built. On the approx. 80 m long running ropes, the guard dogs could only move in this section of the border. About a year later, the first concrete observation towers were erected within sight of the border. Several concrete rings were stacked on top of each other on a concrete fundament and at the upper end was an octagonal observation pulpit with display windows, embrasures and searchlights. These so-called B-towers were partly only a stone's throw away from us and manned day and night by two soldiers.

Starting in the fall of 1970, the self-firing devices (also known as SM-70) were mounted vertically on the border fence, staggered in three rows. They were connected with three tension wires, each of which had its own function. Two of them served to repel game and birds and the middle wire was the actual "trigger". If this was touched by a fugitive, an explosion was triggered and metal splinters were ejected up to a distance of 120 m, which could result in fatal injuries. In addition, a switch indicator in the command tower, which was manned by officers, indicated an alarm.

As a result of negotiations with the Federal Republic, the GDR began removing all ground and fragmentation mines in the fall of 1983, a process that lasted until Oct. 1985. Then in 1984, under pressure from the Federal Government, the SM-70 self-propelled grenades were dismantled and secretly scrapped. At certain intervals, the expanded metal fence also had access gates so that injured people could be rescued and arrested in the event of an unsuccessful escape. Also, in certain places the fastening screws of the panels were only tightened by hand, so that they could easily be dismantled by members of the Stasi in case of smuggling of spies.

The course of the border at the historically significant area along the "Sperrgürtel" was the former state border between Bavaria and Thuringia. It was marked by the old boundary stones. On top it was written: "KB" for Kingdom of Bavaria and "FR" for Principality of Reuss. The border posts of the Bavarian border police were white-blue and those of the GDR had the colors black-red-gold and the emblem of the GDR. The GDR border posts were set back 3 - 5 m from the actual border line.

Former railroad line Lichtenberg- Blankenstein / Thuringia

Today, the former "death strip" is a landscape conservation area. The "Green Belt" runs across Germany to the Baltic Sea. The legendary "Rennsteig" begins in Blankenstein/Thuringia and can now be hiked again as far as Eisenach. In addition, the hiking hub of the Franconian Trail, the Franconian Mountain Trail and the Rennsteig is located here.

The inhabitants of the 5-km restricted area had a stamp in their passport that authorized them to enter and leave the area.

Life inside the five km exclusion zone of the GDR

Along the five km exclusion zone, roadblocks with checkpoints were set up that were constantly manned by People's Police officers. They checked very closely and also harassingly and only those could pass who could show a valid pass. Visiting relatives who lived outside the restricted area was only possible if a resident in the restricted area applied for a temporary residence permit for them and, after much bureaucratic effort, received one. Without such a permit, no visit to the restricted area was possible, not even for a funeral. Non-relatives were not allowed to enter the restricted area at all. But the border inhabitants were inventive there, too.

A former border guard, and now my good friend Günther H. from Sch., told me that he had been called up from his home, the Spreewald, to do his military service at the southern Thuringian border. There he married a local girl from the restricted area and also took up residence there. Since his schoolmates and old friends could never visit him in the Sperrbezirk, he had his children "baptized socialistically" in the Blankenstein Kulturhaus, i.e. the children were not baptized by a priest, but by the party secretary, and he gave a schoolmate or friend as godfather in each case. Thus, they could also visit him in the restricted area.

Furthermore, there were bottlenecks in the supply of food and consumer goods. The HO stores sold mostly home-grown food. It was very rare to find tropical fruits. However, if they were available from time to time, a "socialist queue" formed immediately and "working people" sometimes left their jobs to buy them. But the basic foodstuffs were very cheap, a two-pound loaf of bread cost only 59 pfennigs, which led to bread being fed to pets and then, for example, the barn rabbits fed with it were not eaten themselves, but sold to the HO stores, because they got a lot of money for it because of the prices set by the state. Then one bought back one's own stable hare cheaply at the low price subsidized by the state. Since other goods were also very scarce, a lively barter trade developed. In daily newspapers one could already read: "Exchange tiles for bathtub".

In Blankenstein, directly on the bank of the border river Selbitz, stood the company Kontex and we could look directly into the production rooms from the bank. In this factory, ladies' outerwear for Kaufhof, Quelle, etc. was manufactured for the "West" and then loaded by the state-owned shipping company "Deutrans" and transported to us. Right next door, on the banks of the Saale, was the Rosenthal paper mill, which employed about 1,300 people in GDR times. It was the largest paper mill in the GDR.

Due to the expansion of the border fortifications, more than ten houses were demolished in Blankenstein in 1972 and the residents were relocated. Sometimes the house owners only found out shortly beforehand. Once the pioneers of the border troops drove through a front garden with their bulldozers and I saw how the old house owner was just able to save some flowers and then the bulldozer made its way through her flowerbeds, where the wall was erected days later.

Today, nothing can be seen of it and in place of the "razed" houses there is now a shopping market with a large parking lot.

Escapes from the GDR to the "Golden West"

By the time the border was opened in 1989, around 3.5 million of the approximately 17 million East Germans had left the SED state. By 1988, some 38,000 GDR citizens had fled across the "Green Border," 2,344 of whom were soldiers of the NVA border troops.

From the time the Wall was built in 1961 until 1989, about 75,000 escapes failed and about 60,000 escape plans were uncovered in advance and those involved were severely punished.

It is not known exactly how many people died at the inner-German border and at the Berlin Wall.

Five groups are known from investigated cases:

- Persons who were killed by GDR armed organs or by the border facilities while attempting to escape,

- persons who died in an accident while attempting to escape in the border area,

- persons who died in the border area and for whose death state organs of the GDR were responsible by action or omission

- persons who died as a result of or in connection with the actions of the border authorities,

- border guards who were killed during an escape operation in the border area.

During the first years of service, refugees from the eastern zone came to us almost weekly, mostly during night duty, and they were soaking wet, since they had to cross the natural water borders to Bavaria. At that time, the border fortifications at Blankenstein consisted only of "Spanish horsemen" about 80 cm high and a few watchtowers, since no mines had been laid there because of the buildings near the border, the houses of the village almost reaching the border rivers.

If the escape was successful, the fugitives usually ran to the next property and asked for notification of the police or they were picked up by us during the patrol. At our police station we first dressed them with dry clothes (donated by us, not paid by the state) and gave them something to drink. After establishing the identity, the reason for escape, the written interrogation, a "pick-up report" was written. Most of the refugees gave political and economic conditions as the reason for their flight.

Many had their GDR identity cards, driver's licenses or other documents with them, wrapped in plastic, which made it easier for us to process the case. If a refugee had relatives in the Federal Republic, the escape was reported to the police there by telex with the request to ask them whether they would be willing to take in the refugee. If they were not willing to take him in, or if he had no one, he was forwarded to the reception center in Giessen, where he was accommodated for the time being.

Escaped uniformed persons, such as soldiers of the NVA border troops or soldiers of the Soviet Army, were handed over by us, together with their weapons, to the CID of the border police in Hof and from there subsequently to a civilian military unit of the Americans. Whereby possibly important intelligence could be collected and evaluated. It is not known how many fugitives did not make it and were apprehended and arrested before reaching the border installations.

Once the fugitive was safe with us, he accompanied us to his border crossing point, where in the meantime the GDR border guards were often present and recorded the "crime scene" photographically, in terms of traces, etc., since it was a criminal offense according to the GDR penal code. They often photographed me with a telephoto lens, because in their eyes I was a potential "escape helper". In some cases, where they were not yet sure whether the fugitive had already reached Bavaria, the border alarm was immediately triggered and a "border cordon" was set up. We could recognize this by the fact that hundreds of soldiers stood along a length of 500 to 1000 meters, always within sight of each other, in order to arrest the possibly arriving "border violator".

The escape of Axel S.

On December 18, 1987, I was on night duty from 7:00 p.m. on. At that time, Axel S. was working at the Rosenthal paper mill in Blankenstein, which is located directly on the border river, the Saale. He waited until it got dark and then left his workplace. At that time there was snow and the border installations were brightly lit. He was also aware that there were sharp dogs at dog runs under the bridge of the Saale. He had also noticed that on that day the screen across the Saale was up because of ice, as there had been ice for days. He chose this section of the border for his escape because he thought that the border guards did not expect that someone would try to escape in the middle of the village.

Under the cover of darkness, he crept to the weir. He had his identity cards and documents in a plastic bag in a chest pouch. He also had diving fins with him. He immediately noticed that the current in the direction of the DDR was very strong, so he put on the diving fins. In the water he immediately submerged because of the bright light of the headlights and the barking dogs and swam in the ice-cold water in the direction of the Selbitz confluence.

For him it was also an advantage that the water was very dirty and so it was more difficult for the border guards to recognize him. After he reached the Selbitz, the water became shallower and shallower, which is why he then put himself in the supine position and continued to move away with his heels and hands just below a watchtower until he reached the saving Bavarian shore. On the road there, he first tried to attract the attention of passing motorists. Since no motorist stopped and he was dripping wet, he went to the next house in Unterwolfstein and asked for help.

There he declared to be a refugee from the GDR and was immediately put under the warm shower. In the meantime, the owner of the house informed our office and, together with a colleague, I picked up the fugitive. At the police station, he gave the economic and political conditions in the GDR as the reason for his escape.

Truck "stolen" after escape from the GDR

The paper factory in Blankenstein had a huge chimney made of clinker bricks. Special chimney masons were brought in from all over the GDR for this construction work. The higher the masons got with the building, the better they could see the state border running below them from above and observe the patrol activities of the GDR border guards.

After a bricklayer had analyzed the patrols in detail, he dared to escape through the Saale, because he knew that it would take again until the next patrol would come. When the "coast was clear", he swam through the Saale and reached the Bavarian side unharmed. At that time, there was a road construction site and the workers had already finished work.

After he had "hot-wired" a construction site truck, he drove this vehicle to Bayreuth and reported to the police station there as a fugitive from the GDR. He was handed over to us for processing. When questioned as to why he had taken the truck without authorization, he stated that he first wanted to get as far away from the border as possible. Criminally, there was no theft, since he did not want to take the truck illegally, but only used it to escape. Therefore, it was only a case of "unauthorized use of a motor vehicle", which would have required a criminal complaint from the construction company. After the company learned about the fugitive's occupation, it did not file a criminal complaint and waived prosecution. The opposite was the case. He was immediately employed by them as a special mason.

GDR border guards shoot at refugees

The last escape with the use of firearms by members of the border troops that I know of happened, as far as I can remember, in the last year of the GDR dictatorship on January 6, 1989, at the bridge over the Saale near Blankenstein, where the Selbitz flows into the Saale. At that time, two couples tried to reach the Bavarian shore by swimming through the ice-cold Saale and were shot at by border guards. While one couple reached the rescuing Bavarian shore, the other two were shot and left injured on GDR territory. Only after lying in the freezing cold for about an hour were the injured refugees taken away by a military vehicle.

From a closed to an open border

While on patrol, I was asked by passers-by what my opinion was on how long the border would remain in place. My answer was always that nothing lasts forever, because the Turks only came as far as Vienna, the Romans as far as the Limes and the Nazis even believed in a 1000 year Reich, which only lasted 12 years, and just like that, one day the "Iron Curtain" will be a thing of the past and the inhumane border will fall and we can once again hike here at the beginning of the Rennsteig in Blankenstein on its heights. In order to later make my grandchildren believe that I was also here on "guard duty", I immortalized myself in 1978 with my initials in a fresh concrete foundation on the county road near Blankenstein, because today there is nothing left of the inhumane border there and you are standing in the middle of Europe.

When the border became more permeable in 1989 and Foreign Minister Genscher announced to the GDR citizens in Prague that they could leave the country, the first trains from Prague overloaded with GDR citizens arrived at our main train station in Hof and the people were taken care of by the aid organizations and also by the Bavarian border police. The local population provided food, clothing and living space.

For us, this meant a lot of overtime, because the people had to be helped, since they only had what they were wearing.

At this time, the GDR border guards were already letting the first people leave with their cars for a day trip to Bavaria, and one Sunday I met a man from Zwickau who came to us in Lichtenberg in his "Wartburg" and had to go back again in the evening because he had promised the GDR border guard that he would.

The first big wave of departures then came in November 1989 via the A 9 freeway from the Hirschberg border crossing to Rudolphstein. I was seconded there to reinforce the border crossing together with other police colleagues. Already on the way there, I saw from a distance of about 2 km the car pile-up wrapped in blue exhaust fumes of two-stroke engines, which reached back as far as one could look on GDR territory. The people leaving the country came in such masses that a check of persons or vehicles was no longer carried out. Although it was almost unbearable with car exhaust fumes, the GDR citizens on the Bavarian side were warmly welcomed by the "Franconians" with bananas, tea and mulled wine, with many a tear flowing. That was the first open border crossing here in our service area.

From then on, I always had a few bananas and some chocolate in my briefcase to hand out to children when, for example, their Trabant broke down and their dad spent hours repairing it. From then on, the municipal and city administrations were totally challenged with paying out the welcome money of 100 DM for each GDR citizen. Several times a day, the mayor of Hof collected up to one million DM from the state central bank Hof in a plastic bag and brought the money to the town hall without any guard.

While on night duty at the Rudolphstein border crossing, I received orders around midnight to drive to the state border on the B 173 near Ullitz, since the Hof Border Police Inspectorate had information that the border from Plauen in the direction of Hof was to be opened that very night. Around midnight, I positioned myself and my colleague at the aforementioned spot on the border. There stood a lonely and abandoned house. After some time, the owner of the house opened the window and asked us if something was going on, since police patrols usually only very rarely stop by her house at the end of the world. We told her that the border would probably be opened tonight. The old woman, who had been living at the far end of Bavaria for 45 years and whose garden bordered directly on the zone border, naturally did not want to believe this. We advised her to close the windows, because when the first "Trabants" would roll in, she would certainly need a gas mask because of the two-stroke exhaust fumes. From where we were standing, we could already see the stationary cars with their headlights on, several kilometers away, behind the expanded metal fence in the direction of Plauen, which wanted to drive to the West. Then, at dawn on November 12, 1989, pioneers of the GDR border troops came and cut open the fence with welding torches and poured gravel over the "death strip." Immediately, the convoy of vehicles set off in the direction of Hof.

After the end of our mission, we drove through Hof back to our office. Although it was still dark and very cold, there were already queues of people in front of the Hof town hall who had left via the already open crossing at the A9 to collect their welcome money.

They also stood in front of the town halls in the other communities in their "socialist queue", as they were used to from "over there", and an orderly course of duty was hardly possible anymore.

Then it all went in quick succession, with the opening of the border crossing on the A 72, in the middle of the countryside and far and wide no village, in the direction of Plauen. Since, of course, no checkpoint buildings could be erected so quickly, construction wagons were brought in for us and the sign "Border Police Station" was attached to them. In these wagons we had to work around the clock with gas stoves and no toilets. Sometimes people were so happy that they flung around my neck and cried or decorated our construction wagon with flowers.

On December 2, 1989, the crosswalk on the old railroad embankment between Lichtenberg and Blankenstein near Blech-schmiedtenhammer, which had been closed since 1945, was opened. Even days before, people from both sides of the Wall were waving to each other at Blankenstein. On the Thuringian side, there were gradually more and more people. While I was on duty alone in my provisional border police station in the old construction trailer, on the GDR side about eight members of the GDR border troops and customs were housed in containers. Now it was possible again for old people to walk to their homes as before. But this was only possible with a valid passport, and so it happened that one day an old woman was sent back by the GDR border guards and arrived at my house crying. The reason she was turned back was that she could only show an identity card instead of a passport and that she could not enter the country with it.

Over my field telephone, I told the border guards in a somewhat loud voice that I was now going to "send over" the woman again and that they should let the old lady enter, because she just wanted to see the "Rennsteigsaal" in Blankenstein again, where she had met her husband. These GDR border guards all came from the already open Hirschberg crossing on the A9 and had been assigned to Blankenstein, and of course they couldn't get rid of their harassing style so quickly. Every now and then I gave them to understand that the old times were now over and that we were now in the middle of Europe.

At the same time, the crosswalk at the stand-alone "Krötenmühle" restaurant in the Carlsgrün district of Bad Steben was also opened. There, too, a construction trailer was set up for us as an "office building" of the Bavarian border police and a bridge was built over the Muschwitz. This crossing was mainly used by Schleglers, Seibisers and Bad Stebeners and was only manned until 10:00 pm. Then it happened that the pub visitors had to climb over the closed gate in the border fence of the GDR at night. I was the last person on duty at this crossing on April 9, 1990. At the same time, the crossing at Blechschmiedtenhammer to Blankenstein was also closed.

At Christmas time in 1989, at the confluence of the Selbitz and the Saale, I met a GDR citizen from Markneukirchen who saw the Wall near Blankenstein from the West for the first time and was so deeply impressed that he cried.

The year of the opening of the border in 1989

- May 2: On the Hungarian-Austrian border, Hungarian Foreign Minister Horn ordered the removal of the barbed wire.

- September 11: Opening of the Hungarian state border. During the first three days, about 15,000 Germans enter the Federal Republic via Hungary and Austria.

- October 1: 5,500 GDR refugees from the German Embassy in Prague and 800 from the Embassy in Warsaw arrive in the FRG. The first special train with over 1000 refugees from the embassy in Prague arrives at the main train station in Hof. The refugees are taken care of by the BRK, police and the Frankenwäldlers at the station, in the Freiheitshalle, and in gymnasiums. Some traveled on to friends and relatives and others stayed here and were accommodated by the local population.

- October 3: 7,600 refugees were again waiting in front of the Prague Embassy. After allowing them to leave, the GDR now introduces visa requirements for CSSR travel.

- October 4: Via Dresden, a mass departure from the GDR takes place in barred trains. A total of eight more special trains with almost 8,000 people arrived at the main train station in Hof on this day.

- October 7: Gorbachev told Honecker: "Whoever is late will be punished by life. Honecker had said a few days earlier: "Communism in its course stops neither ox nor donkey". However, he was proven wrong and Gorbachev's statement was then additionally the signal for the opposition in the GDR. In many cities and, to a lesser extent, in the countryside, tens of thousands demonstrated for freedom and reform.

- October 16: In Leipzig alone, more than 12,000 people demonstrated for their rights.

- October 18: The resignation of Erich Honecker was announced in the press at 2:12 p.m.

- November 8: The entire Politburo of the SED resigns in unison. So far, about 50,000 GDR citizens have entered the Federal Republic via the CSSR.

- November 9: Günter Schabowski, Central Committee Secretary for Information, announced to the press in East Berlin at 6:15 p.m. that all GDR citizens could leave the country for West Berlin and the Federal Republic via all border crossings.

- November 9-10: The border crossing on the A 9 Hirschberg is opened. At around 01:45, the first GDR citizens arrive to enter Bavaria.

- November 11: Nearly 120,000 GDR citizens enter the country via the Hof railroad crossing and the Hirschberg/Rudolphstein crossing. Traffic on the access roads to Hof and in the city center collapses. The whole of Hof is effectively a "pedestrian zone" and long lines of people form in front of the payment offices for the 100 DM welcome money. In the supermarkets, coffee, bananas, tuna, peanuts, etc. are sold out and the floors of the markets are covered with snow slush several centimeters high. Only about 100 km from the Franconian Forest towards the south the rush of buyers was no longer so bad and we sometimes shopped in the Bamberg area.

- November 12: That night, the B 173 Hof/Plauen crossing was opened. When I was back home from night duty, I heard on the radio around 9:30 a.m. that the first Trabants and Wartburgs were rolling over this new provisional and only graveled crossing.

- As of January 1, 1990, the border surveillance and people control at the former death strip or iron curtain was completely stopped and on September 1, 1990, the border police station Bad Steben, which had existed until then, was dissolved and incorporated into the Bavarian State Police. The Bavarian Border Police was founded on March 1, 1946 by order of the American occupying power along the Soviet-occupied zone. The main task of the border guards at that time was to prevent and monitor illegal border crossings by people from the Soviet-occupied zone, to check refugees, and to stop smuggling and black market trade. The old colleagues told me that they were hired "off the street", but only if they had a "clean slate". Since there were no uniforms at that time, they simply dyed their old, gray Wehrmacht uniforms black.

Today, border police are only present at the "borderline" between the USA and Mexico, where human trafficking and drug smuggling are to be prevented and illegal immigrants are to be kept away. Thank God there are no mines or self-propelled grenades there to kill people who want to go free.

The new reality

For my colleagues of the border police station Bad Steben I organized an excursion in June 1990 with a trip to the former GDR to the Saale dam and we could travel cheaply and for the first time without visa and minimum exchange of East Mark. Starting from 1 July the D-Mark was introduced. Although I had already planned this trip 6 weeks before and had ordered goose roast with dumplings for 30 people from the landlady of the restaurant "Kranen" in Saalburg, which was located directly on the Saale, we all had to wait at the entrance of the restaurant, because we were "seated", just as it was usual in the GDR, and we did not get our ordered food, but had to make do with barn rabbits. The waitress said that she had not received anything else from the HO-Service and that we should be satisfied with it, there is nothing else.

In the beginning, we were only allowed to give GDR citizens free warnings for traffic violations, but this was gradually abolished, of course. We also turned a blind eye to the traffic safety of their cars. In the meantime, the Trabants and Wartburgs have almost died out and are already being traded as collector's items, and our good Frankenwald air is also back.

Fifty years ago, the construction of the Berlin Wall sealed the division of Germany. Here with us, there was not the "Berlin Wall," but there was a militarily secured, deadly border. Like the wall in Berlin, this divided the region, separated families and friends, cut off watercourses such as the Muschwitz, Selbitz and Saale and road links from the dirt track to the two freeways A9 and A 72.

The barbed wire barriers, which were still very provisional in the beginning, gave way over the years to a barrier system consisting of mines, expanded metal fences, column roads, watchtowers, automatic firing systems and other barrier elements. Since this inhumanity of the border is still a topic of discussion on both sides, on October 3, 2010, consisting of former Bavarian and Thuringian "Grenzern" (border patrol police), the "Grenzerstammtisch" was founded in Carlsgrün, to which I also belong. These former GDR frontiersmen and I have one thing in common, and that is that they as well as I did not come from the Franconian Forest. They came involuntarily from the north of the GDR and had to do their military service in the south, this was so wanted by the regime, so that no kinship relations existed. GDR soldiers were thus ordered to guard the southern border from the Baltic Sea or the Spreewald, for example, and the "Thuringians" had to "stand guard" at the Baltic Sea or the Berlin Wall. During this time of border duty, both the then young border guards and I got to know our wives living in the border area, got married here and "stuck" here. This is what happened to many young men on both sides of the border.

We cannot tell you about stories of the Berlin Wall, but we can tell you about countless events and incidents we experienced ourselves on the inner-German border right on our doorstep, such as the order to shoot, smuggling, spies, dead mailboxes, mine victims, etc., and of course about successful escapes, such as the legendary hot-air balloon flight of two families with their children. This escape was even filmed as a feature film under the title "With the Wind to the West".

We Stammtisch members from West and East sit together once a month, each time in a different village in the Wirtshaus, over there and over here in convivial company. We are former Bavarian border police officers, West German customs officers, GDR People's Police officers and soldiers of the NVA border troops, as well as other contemporary witnesses. We tell self-experienced German-German border stories and want to preserve history.

Since we also want to be funny and cheerful, we sing from time to time a song "Jenseits des Tales" ("Beyond the Valley"), re-penned by our singing brother, Werner Engelhardt:

Beyond the valley were dugouts

To the high evening sky the smoke was billowing, that was a singing in the wide field and many border soldiers were singing too.

They diligently cleaned their old weapons

But one beauty did not fade from mind

And while they were singing, one of the border guards said:

"Men, you know where the youngest went"?

On this side of the valley stood the youngest frontiersman

And grasped the damp earth from the bottom

It did not cool the embers of his poor forehead

It did not make his sick heart well

He was held only by two youthful cheeks

And only one mouth, which he forbade to himself

Even more tightly the youngest closed his lips

And looked across into the evening glow

Beyond the valley were dugouts

From the red evening sky the smoke was billowing, there was laughter in the wide field and that border guard, he laughed too.

From Blankenstein to Nordhalben there are countless of these border experiences on the Bavarian and Thuringian side, which did not always end happily. It is important to us to keep the past in memory and to pass it on, because one day the generations and contemporary witnesses will no longer be there and our children and young people will no longer know anything about the inhumane division of Germany. That is why I have already been to schools in Bavaria and Thuringia and have given lectures about this inhuman border to students who were born after the fall of the Wall in 1989.

Stories and incidents on the border between East and West

The balloon escape

The GDR citizen Peter Strelzyk from Pößneck/Thuringia. had come up with a special escape plan. He planned to escape with his wife and two children in a homemade hot air balloon. His friend and colleague at the plastics manufacturer VEB Polymer in Pößneck heard about it and was enthusiastic about the escape plan. In their spare time, they both secretly welded together the burner and the "basket" in their cellar, which was not a basket but a platform of only 1.40 m x 1.40 m, with posts 80 cm high at each of the four corners, which were connected to each other with clotheslines. These lines were the only protection for Peter Strelzyk, his work colleague Günter Wetzel, their wives Doris and Petra and their four children.

With their wives, they sewed together the different colored fabrics they had previously bought together all over the GDR, using an old sewing machine. They had to be careful even when buying the fabric, because in the former GDR it was not easy to buy several meters of fabric just like that. Firstly, this would have been noticed by the sales staff and possibly reported to the Stasi, and secondly, so much fabric was not available for sale. In order not to attract attention, they therefore only ever purchased smaller quantities. In total, they procured about 1200 square meters of tent, clothing, and umbrella fabric, from which they finally created a balloon about 28 meters high and 20 meters wide.

On September 16, 1979, shortly after midnight, the two families from Pößneck arrived with their Wartburg and a trailer near the border on a forest meadow. After unloading the colorful balloon envelope weighing about 100 kg, the burner, the platform and four propane gas bottles, the balloon was inflated with the help of a converted 14 HP motorcycle engine. In the process, the balloon envelope caught fire and the escape seemed to fail. But with a fire extinguisher Peter Strelzyk managed to put out the fire of the envelope. Now everyone stood on the platform with their backs to the outside and held on to the gas cylinders standing in the middle. After they had ascended about 2500 meters, the north wind carried them over the barriers to the south west past Lichtenberg, and after a breathtaking 28-minute flight they landed somewhat ungently in a wooded area near Naila in the district of Finkenflug near a farm. Since the night was very bright due to the moon, they noticed that at the end they "drove" over many small fields, whereas in the GDR there were mainly very large fields. Hope arose that they might have made it.

Next, the two men walked to a high-voltage pylon whose nameplate said something about "Überlandwerk," which they didn't know from the GDR. After they had gone further, they came to the nearby farm. Before that, the women and the children had first to hide in the bushes. In the barn, the two men then saw an agricultural machine standing there and they now knew, based on the type, that they had made it.

When they came out of the barn again, they saw two headlights coming towards them and heard engine noise. Then a car pulled up in front of them and two West German police officers got out. One of the two fugitives asked the officers: "Are we in the West here?" to which one of the police officers replied: "Of course, where else". Now it was finally clear to them that they were in the West. With firecrackers they signaled to their hidden wives and children that they could now come out of hiding.

The two police officers were Rudolf G. and his patrol partner H. from the Naila police station. During the night patrol they saw the "fireball" in the sky from far away and could not explain the unknown flying object at all and drove after the "UFO" for safety's sake.

After the landing, I was informed about the flight by my office at about 6:30 a.m. and then drove to the landing site together with my colleague Alfred F., since we as border police were responsible for the processing of the fugitives. A feature film was later made about this escape with the title "With the Wind to the West". The two families made the escape balloon available to the general public. The platform with the gas cylinders is in the local history museum in Naila and the balloon envelope is in a museum in Berlin.

While the Strelzyks settled in Bad Kissingen and opened an electrical store there, the Wetzels stayed here in the Franconian Forest for the time being and later moved to the vicinity of Bayreuth.

After the fall of the Wall and the collapse of the GDR, the Strelzyk couple returned to their old house in Pößneck in the mid-1990s.

Today the two families no longer have any contact with each other.

The author of the book after the successful landing in front of the hot air balloon of the refugees

Chicken bones from West to East

The GDR also had a state-owned forwarding agency with the company name "DEUTRANS", which transported furniture, clothes, meat, brown coal, live cattle, broken glass, etc. from East to West. According to our findings, these trucks were predominantly driven by Stasi and military members of the NVA, disguised as long-distance drivers in civilian clothes. During these journeys, they were also tasked with spying on intelligence and military information in the Federal Republic.

In our area, for example, they drove specifically to the Bundeswehr barracks in Naila and feigned tire or engine failures there. In the process, they photographed the interior of the barracks through a small hole in the body or tarpaulin. They also drew maps of the explosion chambers for emergencies, which were hidden in the roadways and camouflaged with a normal manhole cover. These were always located where there was either a large river or steeply sloping terrain and where, in the event of an emergency, the Warsaw Pact's military machinery was to be stopped after the blast.

During their stay with us, of course, they did not despise capitalist prosperity and enjoyed everything they did not get "over there." No matter if it was tropical fruits, the magazine "Playboy" or other magazines. So that they would not be caught on their return, they disposed of these things, which were "forbidden" to them, in the wastebaskets at the rest areas of the A 9 shortly before the border crossing at Rudolphstein.

Because West German and Berlin citizens were also always frisked and harassed by their security agencies at the Hirschberg border crossing, the "Western" border guards sometimes threw the remains of a roast chicken on top of the tarpaulins of their trucks. Since we knew that their border guards with German shepherd dogs "sniffed" the incoming motor vehicles for people, we knew that the dogs would smell the bones and of course attack the trucks like wild lions, since the sniffer dogs smelled the bones and the GDR border guards then thought that people were hidden in the vehicle. That must have caused trouble and we grinned gleefully.

Smuggling of GDR citizens to the West by small plane

On May 21, 1983, at about 8:45 a.m., a West German sports plane was strafed by Russian helicopters northwest of Hof near Bad Steben and hit by several projectiles. The helicopters were located near the restaurant "Krötenmühle", OT Carlsgrün, at an altitude of 50 to 100 meters. The pilot just managed to shake off the pursuers and fly low over the demarcation line to the west. The aircraft must have been in GDR airspace for a long time, since helicopters can usually only arrive at a certain point after about 60 minutes. So much for a report in a newspaper.

What happened on this Whitsun Saturday? A West German pilot had borrowed a sports plane from Fulda and within a year had made several flights across the zone border into the GDR, landing briefly on meadows near the town of Pößneck, picking up GDR citizens willing to leave the country and then smuggling them into the West.

On this day, he wanted to pick up people again and found out during the landing procedure that the grass was too high at the agreed meeting point and therefore a landing was not possible. Therefore, he took off again and flew back in the direction of Bavaria.

But someone had betrayed his escape help to the Stasi. Even before he reached the zone border, two Russian MI 24 attack helicopters were waiting for him. They immediately fired rockets and machine guns at his Piper PA 18 with the registration number "D-EHCK". Despite several bullet holes in his plane, he was able to reach Bavaria in low-level flight and then flew on via Carlsgrün and Steinbach to his airfield in Fulda-Jossa. There he parked the aircraft, which he had rented from an aviation club. Since this illegal flight in the ADIZ zone (a zone closed to normal air traffic along the Iron Curtain) had also come to the attention of the air traffic control at the airfield in Hof, the pilot was visited three days later by the criminal police in his home town of Tuttlingen and questioned about it.

On that day, the GDR's "Neues Deutschland" also published a harsh indictment of the "airspace violator" and his "provocative" actions. The entire "operation" lasted just under two hours, from takeoff near Fulda to the return of the aircraft. According to eyewitness reports from Carlsgrün citizens, the Russian attack helicopters flew over Carlsgrün and into Bavarian airspace. Bullets did not hit our area because the helicopter pilots had orders to shoot in the direction of Thuringia.

From the former border guards from Schlegel and Seibis, who belong to our border regulars' table, I only learned in 2010 that several bullets hit rabbit hutches during the shooting in the village of Lichtenbrunn near the border and that some animals lost their lives. The owners of the animals did not dare to file damage claims with the GDR authorities at that time and have therefore not received any compensation to this day.

Escape with agricultural plane

In the GDR, there were also the "agricultural planes" which sprayed the large fields of the LPG with fertilizer or pesticides. One day, in the 1980s, a pilot fled from Thuringia to Bavaria in his rickety aircraft. After finishing his work, he flew to the nearby A9 Berlin-Munich highway to use it as an orientation to the south. With the Autobahn always below him, he flew low over the GDR border crossing at

Hirschberg and then over the Bavarian border crossing at Rudolphstein. Shortly after the Bavarian crossing, he made an emergency landing in a meadow near the village of Moos and was immediately welcomed as a fugitive by Bavarian "border guards". Our mission was to guard the aircraft, which was the property of the GDR, until it had been dismantled in such a way that it could be driven back to the GDR by truck and handed over there. It was returned to the GDR via the Saale Bridge.

Border near Blechschmiedtenhammer, on top of the hill bunker of the border guards of the NVA border troops

West Germans as Spies

A local border resident spied for the East Zone. Since he had grown up here, he knew the area like the back of his hand and always walked through the Höllental to the border. To avoid running into a patrol of us, the customs officers or the BGS, he carried a radio from the GDR. The Stasi had taken up residence in the attic of a house in Blankenstein, right next to the border, and from there they could keep a close eye on our patrols with binoculars. When we moved away from the border into the hinterland again, they radioed this to the spy and thus he was able to cross the small border stream of Muschwitz at Blechschmiedtenhammer safely and without difficulty and was taken over there by the already waiting Stasi members.

As he told us later after his arrest, this even worked in the dark of night, because our patrols always had to cross a railroad crossing in this area and at these crossings, a light was on all through the night and thus we could be seen in the light when we moved away from the border again and the coast was clear for the spy. As he also was a professional bus driver he used several times the possibility of depositing spy material on parking lots in the GDR in TBK (dead letter boxes) on his way to Berlin on the "Transit Autobahn". He was later sentenced to prison for his espionage.

High-ranking police officer exposed as a spy

In the 1980s, a spy who was still in custody agreed to participate in an educational film on espionage for the police and other services. For this reason, he was transferred from Hesse to the Hof correctional facility by way of the Schubwesen system. From there he was transported daily by police car to and from the filming location "Ullsteinpark" near Lichtenberg, which directly bordered the zone border. Our main task was to prevent him from jumping over the border stream there, which was only one or two meters wide, into the GDR, because he would have been granted asylum there. During breaks in filming, he told me how he had been recruited by the Stasi for their purposes.

According to him, everything began quite inconspicuously. He was still a high school student and often visited his grandmother in the former

GDR during the vacations. At a dance, he was approached by a man from State Security, who told him that he could come to the GDR much more often and that he could help him obtain the necessary visas. This man also often paid him the bill. After a few years, he signed a declaration of commitment to this man for the State Security Service. It was not until he was about to graduate from high school that the Stasi leadership officer contacted him again and insisted that he study law and would also receive regular money during his studies.

After graduation, his commanding officer demanded that he apply for a job in the Bavarian police for higher service. At that time, the Stasi wrote his application on an electric typewriter so that it would look good. But that didn't help either, because probably because of his relatives in the GDR he wasn't hired by the state of Bavaria. Now the Stasi wrote a new application for him to the Federal Border Guard and it worked. He was hired into the higher service with his law degree and was ordered by East Berlin to photograph secret documents of his office and smuggle them across the green border into the GDR or to hide them in a TBK right at the zone border. But first he had to learn from the Stasi how to take secret photographs with a mini camera built into an electric razor.

For this reason, he took the train several times from his home in Nuremberg, disguised as a hiker, to the border area via Hof main station and continued by train in the direction of Bad Steben to the Hölle stop. There he got off the train and walked through the Höllental valley. If he had been subjected to a personal check by us, he would not have been noticed, since he was equipped with a duplicate of a federal identity card of another existing, uncollared federal citizen, and in our customs border district every citizen was allowed to go as far as the actual border.

After the Höllental, he turned right at the restaurant "Blechschmiedtenhammer" and then went into the "Ullsteinpark", through which the border stream Muschwitz ran. There, at a narrow spot, he jumped over the stream and was already on GDR territory, where he was already met by Stasi members disguised in uniforms of the GDR border troops. A uniform coat and a cap were immediately thrown over him so that it looked as if he were one of them and then he was quickly driven away in the waiting military jeep on the column road so that we would not notice anything. Before that, of course, the normal border patrols and watchtower crews had been withdrawn to the hinterland in this section of the border so that they, too, would not learn of the agent smuggling.

He made this trip from Nuremberg to us several times and always crossed the green border. Of course I wanted to know why he always used the train as a means of transportation and why he did not enter the GDR by car via the border crossing on the A 9, when he would not have attracted attention with his identity papers. He told me that if he had used his car, he might have broken down or run into a police checkpoint, and that his smuggling officers would have had to wait for him. In addition, the smuggling was much safer and not so stressful, because he would have been checked at the Rudolphstein border crossing and would have suffered sweating before the check.

After several years of visiting his office with a miniature camera hidden in his razor and photographing secret documents, he revealed himself to his wife. She asked a clergyman for advice and both of them then filed a self-denunciation with the CID. After the shooting was completed, he had to serve his remaining sentence. It is not known whether he was granted remission for agreeing to show his smuggling activities in an educational film.

One of the first wooden watchtowers near Blankenstein. Today the Rennsteig begins there on a new bridge

April Fool's Jokes

On April 1, our office came up with the idea of teasing the GDR border guards:

We built a frame that a colleague strapped to his back. At the back it looked like the turbine of a helicopter and from there a drive shaft went up to a rotor, of course all made of cardboard and wood. Equipped with this dummy we went on foot patrol. As we approached the concrete observation tower near Blankenstein, separated only by the narrow border river, we saw that the GDR border guards were frantically grabbing binoculars and pointing them at us. One of the soldiers hurriedly picked up the field telephone and reported to his unit that the "Bavarians" were now already equipped with one-man helicopters.

Reunification" celebrated with a handshake as early as 1981:

Of course, we also had uniforms and Kalashnikovs from escaped NVA border soldiers in our evidence room.

Then we had the idea to annoy the border authorities of the GDR once again on April 1. For this purpose, a colleague of mine put on a GDR uniform and armed himself with a Kalashnikov machine pistol. Then we drove to the border to a place where the manned observation tower was only a few meters away from us and took pictures of the alleged "NVA border guard" and a Bavarian border guard as they were shaking hands and hugging. The border guards on the watchtower could not hide their amazement and did not know how it could happen that they were still locked up behind the fence and that on the Bavarian side a colleague of theirs was fraternizing with the "Bavarians".

This photo was printed after agreement with the local daily newspaper "Frankenpost" naturally on April 1 with the title: "The reunification makes progress: GDR border guards and Bavarian border guards greet each other warmly". Surely an agent then had to create a copy of this newspaper and hand it over to the Stasi.

Red water in the border river

Sometime in the spring, during a border patrol, I noticed that the border river "Selbitz" was carrying red colored water. Since I knew that the GDR was discharging Selbitz water for the paper mill located in Blankenstein, I knew that I would inform the GDR border guards about it.

On that day, two workers from the GDR Water Management Office were working directly on the banks of the Selbitz River, guarded, as always, by several GDR soldiers. I approached these men and called out to the border guards that red Selbitz water was flowing from Bavaria in the direction of the GDR and that they should pass on this message via their field telephone. However, they made no effort to do anything and showed no reaction, nor did they give me any answer, which was not surprising when you know that they were not allowed to talk to the "class enemy". Only when I became more harsh and warned them that red "communist" paper would then be produced in the paper mill and they would have to bear the consequences, did one of them report the incident further. It should be noted that at that time, white paper was produced in this largest paper mill in the GDR by about 1300 workers, mainly for export to the Federal Republic.

Three meter high concrete wall near the village of Blankenstein / Thuringia

Unbureaucratic border traffic

In our border section there was a pub directly at the zone border. For more than 100 years, the pub's own deep well for drinking water had been located on Thuringian territory and thus, after the division of Germany, on GDR territory. In the event of a defect or other malfunction in the pumping station or the pipeline, the pub-keeper went to the border and called out to the GDR border guards: "Listen, my water isn't running, I have to check the well to see what the problem is," and the soldiers answered him from the watchtower: "Yes, you can come over here".

This was the unbureaucratic way of doing things for decades, and the pub-keeper even gave the border guards a snack in return. This changed with the erection of the expanded metal fence, since the way to the well had been blocked for the landlord. Now, in case of a disturbance of his water, he would have had to inform our office first and then we would have had to ask for permission from the border troops at the opposite border control point Hirschberg via the so-called "red telephone" from the border crossing Rudolphstein. This procedure was then too cumbersome for the landlord and he finally gave up his well.

How we helped GDR pensioners to travel the big world

Pensioners from the GDR were allowed to visit relatives in the Federal Republic upon request. In certain cases, such as weddings, bereavements, etc., it was even possible for married GDR citizens to travel to the West, but one spouse had to stay at home and they carried only their GDR identity card with them.

As soon as they entered Bavaria, our border officials told them how they could travel to Africa, Asia, America or the rest of the world during their stay in the West. Since they did not have a passport, but only their GDR identity card, which of course was not recognized anywhere, they received, since they were German citizens, a German passport from a municipal administration in our service area and could, alone or also with their relatives or friends, travel the whole world with this passport. However, they had to return it to this municipal administration after the end of their trip so that the GDR authorities would not "get wind" of it. Until their next visit to the West, the passport was officially kept and they could get it back at any time. To ensure their trip could start right away it happened sometimes that such a passport was issued even at night or on weekends due to our good relations with the town hall staff.

Russian Tanks Drive Towards the West

An old woman from a small border town in our service area had very good relations with politicians in Munich. Her house was only about 500 meters from the border. One day in summer, she heard loud engine noise coming from Thuringia, which was getting closer and closer. Instead of informing our police station, she picked up the phone and called the Ministry of the Interior in Munich and told them that Russian tanks were on their way to Bavaria and that we were under attack. Since the situation center there was not yet aware of any "outbreak of war" on the part of the GDR, they immediately telephoned our office and demanded immediate reporting with the remark: "Why don't you know anything up there in Upper Franconia about a mobilization of the GDR People's Army, you must be asleep". Therefore, a patrol was immediately ordered to the border. They quickly discovered that several combine harvesters from the Schlegel agricultural cooperative had begun harvesting grain and were driving in a single line across the large fields. Since there were Soviet "Progress" combine harvesters, they sounded somewhat louder than ours. After the "Munichers" were informed accordingly by us, they calmed down again.

Border guards of the GDR enter Bavarian territory

From my acquaintance, the customs officer Egon H., I learned the following: During a foot patrol in the forest area "Krötensee" he found a patrol leader control book of the NVA border troops about 300 meters from the border on Bavarian territory. Only a patrol leader had such a control book with him, because it contained the radio call names and coded texts of the patrols, etc., which were not allowed to fall into the hands of the "class enemy".

Why the GDR border guard lost this secret book on the Bavarian side and why he crossed the border at all is a matter of speculation. Possibly it was an unsuccessful escape and the border guard ran after the fugitive and dragged him back into the GDR, losing his patrol book in the process. In any case, this again proved that the soldiers of the GDR border troop, when there were no patrols nearby from our side, crossed the border to Bavaria, pursued fugitives, arrested them on Bavarian soil and dragged them back into the GDR.

Scouting party of border troop sneaks into Bavarian territory

In the summer vacations of 1982, my 14-year-old son and his best friend Markus R. rode their bicycles to the zone border to build a "little house" in the forest. For this project they took an axe, saw, hammer, pliers and whatever else was needed. The best place for them was a piece of forest near the former butter mill near Lichtenberg. About 50 meters away from the border stream Thüringer Muschwitz. Directly opposite in approx. 200 meters distance was a constantly occupied and with branches camouflaged earth bunker of the GDR border troops.

After they had been felling weak, scrawny trees with their tools for several days and had not exactly been silent in the process, the border guards opposite them in their earth bunker naturally became aware of them. Since these border guards could not look themselves because of the intervening mine belt, they informed their border company in the village of Schlegel of the "suspicious" knocking noises from the forest. Presumably they suspected that Bavarian border guards or customs officers were also building a shelter there, which could have been the case, since there were indeed wooden customs officers' houses along the zone border at certain intervals, where they could shelter in bad weather.

One day, the two children were again fully engaged in their "construction work," when suddenly six to eight soldiers of the GDR border troop in camouflage uniforms stood directly behind them and took pictures of them and their almost completed "little house." The children were so frightened that they even abandoned their new bicycles and ran two kilometers uphill to

Lichtenberg. Breathing heavily, they then informed our border police station, where I was on duty, about the "border incident" from a public telephone booth.

After I had told them to wait at the telephone booth, I drove there with a colleague, loaded them into the staff car and drove to the border. Before that, my office manager had said: "I don't believe that the GDR border guards are entering Bavarian territory, those are children's fantasies". Of course, when we arrived at the border creek, the soldiers had crept back through the Muschwitz into GDR territory, and far and wide there was no one to be seen. But then my son said: "Dad, they took our pliers, which were lying here on the forest floor near our "little house". But their two bicycles were still there.

Together we went back to the official car and I called over the border: "It is sad that you are already so poor that you have to "steal" my pliers". At that moment the tall grass in front of the expanded metal fence shook and the soldiers of the patrol got up and ran through a gate in the fence back towards the interior and I felt confirmed again that the GDR border guards do enter Bavarian soil when the "coast is clear".

It should be noted that the soldiers had entered through a locked gate and there were no mines there. Such gates were installed at certain intervals so that members of the border troops could retrieve the fugitive from the death strip in the event of an unsuccessful escape, or for border reconnaissance officers who also had a key for them. The ordinary soldier had to run behind the expanded metal fence and of course had no key for the gate, because there was the danger that he could escape as well.

Probably the soldiers of the scouting party, on their return to their barracks, joyfully showed their booty, my pliers, to the company commander. He was probably not so pleased, because the next day a patrol of the Federal Border Guard found my pliers again on Bavarian territory, deposited on a turnpike, directly at the border stream Muschwitz. Since it was not an everyday occurrence for a BGS patrol to find such an object while on patrol, the young border guards thought about it and, as a precautionary measure, first secured them and took them back to their barracks in Bayreuth, since the pliers could have been left behind during an as yet unknown or unsuccessful escape.

The next day, our border police station received a telex from the Bayreuth Federal Border Guard reporting the discovery of pliers at the border near Lichtenberg and asking whether we knew anything about an escape. In my reply, I informed the unit there that the find was my pliers, which had been taken by the GDR border guards and then put back on the turnpike. A few days later, a BGS patrol visited me at our office and handed over my pliers. Thus ended the round trip of a Bavarian pair of pliers across the death strip into the GDR and back again.

Refugee's foot is torn off by mine and remains severely injured in death strip

Some refugees were very lucky and crossed the death strip without being injured. But others had no guardian angel with them and remained seriously injured in the mine belt or were possibly killed. However, I am not aware of any refugees who were killed in our service area.

However, my colleagues told me that in September 1963 in a dark night in the forest area "Kroetensee" a teacher with his two 10- to 12-year-old children tried to cross the mine belt at the "Neundorfer Sperre". In the process, a mine went off, tore off his foot, and he was left severely injured. He sent his uninjured children on and asked them to get help in the next village. After several kilometers and wandering in the forest, the children came to the road Langenbach-Heinersberg, where they caught the eye of the car driver Erwin H..

After they told the driver that their father had been seriously injured in the mine belt during the escape, he picked up the children and drove them to the border police station in Bad Steben and delivered them there. Together with the car driver who had picked up the children and the country doctor, Dr. Konitzer, a patrol crew with two colleagues drove back to the forest area. There, the children first had to find the border crossing again, which was not easy at night, and guide the border guards to where their injured father lay.

In the meantime, he had tied off the bleeding stump of his leg with his trouser belt. The explosion also drew the attention of the GDR border guards to the escape and they ran in the direction of the explosion site. Since they themselves could not go to the injured man in the mine belt, they shouted to him to return to GDR territory. When our border guards then arrived, they announced over outside loudspeakers: " This is the Bavarian Border Police" and the border guards fired their Kalashnikovs into the air, shouting several times: "Do not enter our territory leave the "border violator" lying there". However, the officer of the Bavarian border police Alfred F. took heart and, risking his life, nevertheless crawled to the injured man and pulled him over to Bavarian territory. There the fugitive was immediately given emergency care by the doctor present and then taken by official car to the district hospital in Naila, where he was then operated on and given further medical care. After several years, this former fugitive visited the Bad Steben border police station again and thanked the officers for rescuing him. He told them that he was working again as a teacher in West Germany and that his wounds had healed well.

GDR border guard shoots Italian truck driver

On August 5, 1976, the Italian truck driver Benito Corghi drove on the A9 from the direction of Berlin to the Hirschberg border crossing in the GDR and, after clearing the border without any problems, continued on to the Rudolphstein border crossing. Once there, he was told by a truck driver who had followed him that he had left "papers" behind during the check in the GDR. To retrieve his documents, he left his truck in Bavaria and walked back across the Saale Bridge in heavy fog, heading for the first checkpoint in the GDR. There, a border guard yelled at the unsuspecting Italian to stop immediately. Since the latter did not understand the request and turned around and ran back in the direction of the Bavarian border crossing at Rudolphstein, the GDR border guard made use of his firearm and hit the truck driver in the back, whereupon he died within a few minutes.

In the press one could read that the Italian government protested sharply and the shot Italian Corghi was even a member of the Italian Communist Party, whereupon the GDR also apologized. This incident was indignantly debated in the Western press for weeks. On August 11, 1976, the widow of the killed man expressed herself in the newspaper "Die Welt": "What happened is the result of an absurd and unacceptable way of defending socialism. We, my children and I," she continued, who was also a communist, "have paid a price that is high, too high. You don't defend socialism with murders."

Epilogue

I did not regard the people in the GDR as enemies and also not the ordinary border guards of the NVA border troops, who were only doing their compulsory military service, but as our German brothers and sisters. In contrast, in the GDR, even the smallest children in kindergarten were educated in such a way that we were the "class enemy" for them.

After more than 42 years of police service and eight promotions up to the rank of Chief Superintendent, I was to retire at the age of 60 in 2005 (the working life of a police officer generally ends at the age of 60). However, since I was a "gendarme" with all my heart and soul, I applied for an extension of my working life by one year. After the application was approved, I was then given a well-deserved retirement in May 2006.

Considering the situation at that time, it was a good decision that I joined the police. I am satisfied, I do not regret it. I enjoyed my job. You got to meet a lot of people and experience a lot. In my learned profession as a butcher, I would certainly never have been so satisfied.

Now that I'm retired, when I look at how the police are regarded today or how young police officers work, I think of my instructor, whose motto was: "Nothing is so good that it can't be improved". In the past, police officers were respected and greeted from afar. That's why I'm not sad that my son didn't become a policeman, but is employed as a civil servant in the computer center of the Deutsche Bundesbank in Munich.

URKUNDE

Gemäß Art. 55 Abs. 6 des Bayerischen Beamtengesetzes tritt

Herr Polizeihauptkommissar

Otto Oeder

mit Ablauf des Monats Mai 2006

nach 1-jähriger Verlängerung

in den Ruhestand.

Für die dem Freistaat Bayern geleisteten Dienste

spreche ich ihm den Dank

der Bayerischen Staatsregierung aus.

Bayreuth, 3. Februar 2006

FÜR DEN BAYERISCHEN STAATSMINISTER
DES INNERN
DAS POLIZEIPRÄSIDIUM OBERFRANKEN

Bauer
Polizeipräsident

Certificate of appreciation from the Free State of Bavaria for services rendered and retirement after approved one-year extension of working life